S0-EAY-414

MODEL
ROCKETS

GREGORY VOGT

MODEL ROCKETS

LARAMIE JR. HIGH IMC
1355 N. 22nd
LARAMIE, WY 82070

**ILLUSTRATED BY
ANNE CANEVARI GREEN**

Franklin Watts
New York | London | Toronto | Sydney | 1982
A First Book

Cover photograph by Ginger Giles,
with special thanks to
Mr. Robert Calandra of Polk's Hobby Department Store.

Photographs courtesy of Estes Industries:
opp. title page and page 1;
and NASA: pp. 4, 11, and 12.

Diagrams on pages 62, 64, and 71
courtesy of Centuri Engineering Co.

Library of Congress Cataloging in Publication Data

Vogt, Gregory.
Model rockets.

(A First book)
Includes index.
Summary: Discusses the history, principles,
and practical aspects of rocketry; presents
experiments that illustrate rocket principles;
and explains how to participate in model rocketry.
1. Rockets (Aeronautics)—Models—
Juvenile literature.
(1. Rockets (Aeronautics)—Models.
2. Models and modelmaking)
I. Green, Anne Canevari, ill. II. Title.
TL844.V63   629.47'5   82-7004
ISBN 0-531-04467-X   AACR2

CONTENTS

For Donna McGarry,
the best teacher I know

MODEL
ROCKETS

INTRODUCTION

Rockets are one of the oldest forms of self-powered vehicles in existence. Forerunners to the rocket were in use more than two thousand years ago. Over a long and exciting history, rockets have evolved into mighty vehicles capable of launching spacecraft that can travel out into the galaxy beyond our solar system. Few experiences can compare with the excitement and thrill of watching a rocket-powered vehicle such as the Space Shuttle thunder into space.

It is only natural that people of all ages want to take part in rocketry, from building a rocket to flying it, but to successfully produce giant vehicles such as the Space Shuttle requires thousands of scientists and engineers working together over many years. There is, however, an alternative to these large rockets—model rockets.

Model rockets are real, not imitations. They work because they use real engines and produce flights that differ from those of giant rockets only in magnitude.

Over the last twenty-five years, model rocketry has grown tremendously in popularity. Supplies for building rockets and commercially produced engines (model rocketeers never build their own engines because of the many dangers in doing so) are readily available at reasonable cost. You can get them at hobby shops, through mail order catalogs, and at toy stores, although model rockets are not really toys. With these supplies, rockets can be built that produce dramatic flights, achieve speeds of hundreds of miles per hour, and return to the ground for future flights.

While it is possible to get started on building rockets without a book, because instructions come with model kits, people who take the time to explore the subject will be "light-years" ahead of those who don't. As you will learn, there is much more to model rocketry than slapping together the rocket's parts. Knowledgeable rocketeers have the advantage of thousands of years of rocketry experience on their side, and their rockets consistently outperform rockets built by others.

CHAPTER 1

THE HISTORY
OF ROCKETS

On the morning of April 12, 1981, in Cape Canaveral, Florida, the most complicated and advanced flying machine ever devised stood ready for its first test flight into space. The Space Shuttle *Columbia*, a combination of rocket and airplane, was about to open a new era in space exploration. As the world's first true spaceship, the Shuttle would take off as a rocket, travel in orbit as a spacecraft, and return to the earth as an ordinary glider (unpowered airplane).

The countdown clocks approached zero. Hundreds of thousands of people lined the Florida beaches and roadways to watch the event, and millions more around the world watched on television sets. Suddenly, billowing clouds of white smoke shot outward and upward from the base of the rocket. The three main engines on the orbiter were gulping liquid hydrogen and oxygen from a large external tank. Then the two solid rocket boosters fired. Orange flames erupted from their nozzles, and spectators had to squint at their brilliance. It was as though two new suns had just been born.

The Space Shuttle *Columbia* at blast-off

Just after 7 A.M. Eastern Standard Time, the Space Shuttle lifted off the launch platform on a giant pillar of orange flames and white smoke. In just eleven minutes, the *Columbia* orbiter reached earth orbit.

The first test flights of the new Space Shuttle and the many flights that will undoubtedly follow are a natural outgrowth of literally thousands of years of experimentation and research on rockets and rocket propulsion.

One of the first devices to successfully employ the principles essential to rocket flight was a wooden bird. In the writings of Aulus Gellius, a Roman, there is a story of a Greek named Archytas who lived in the city of Tarentum, now a part of southern Italy. Somewhere around the year 400 B.C., Archytas mystified and amused the citizens of Tarentum by flying a pigeon made of wood. It appears that the bird was suspended on wires and propelled along by escaping steam. The pigeon used the action-reaction principle that was not to be stated as a scientific law until the seventeenth century.

About three hundred years after the pigeon, another Greek, Heron of Alexandria, invented a similar device called an *aeolipile*. It, too, used steam as a propulsive gas. Heron mounted a sphere on top of a water kettle. A fire below the kettle turned the water into steam, and the gas traveled through pipes to the sphere. Two L-shaped tubes on opposite sides of the sphere allowed the gas to escape, and in so doing gave a thrust to the sphere.

A thousand years elapsed. The first date we know of when rockets were used was the year 1232. At this time, the Chinese and the Mongols were at war with each other. During the battle of Kai-Feng, the Chinese repelled the Mongol invaders by a barrage of "arrows of flying fire." These fire-arrows were a simple form of solid-propellant rocket. A tube, capped at one end, was filled with a remarkable chemical mixture that would come to be known as gunpowder. The other end was left open, and the tube was attached to a long stick. When the powder was ignited, the rapid burning of the powder produced fire, smoke, and gas that escaped out the open end and produced a thrust. The stick acted as a simple guidance system that kept the rocket headed in one general direction as it flew through the air.

Although the first recorded use of true rockets was in 1232, rockets must have been developed years earlier, possibly in the eleventh century. The invention of gunpowder goes even farther back in history.

In the first century A.D., the Chinese were reported to have had a simple form of gunpowder made from saltpeter, sulfur, and charcoal dust. It was used mostly for fireworks in religious and other festive celebrations.

The next important step in developing rockets was to attach bamboo tubes filled with gunpowder to arrows and launch them with bows. Soon it was discovered that these gunpowder tubes could launch themselves just by the power produced from the escaping gas. The true rocket was born.

Following the battle of Kai-Feng, the Mongols produced rockets of their own and may have been responsible for the spread of rockets to Europe. All through the thirteenth to the fifteenth centuries there were reports of many rocket experiments. In England, a monk named Roger Bacon worked on improved forms of gunpowder that greatly increased the range of rockets. In France, Jean Froissart found that more accurate flights could be achieved by launching rockets through tubes. Froissart's idea was the forerunner of the modern bazooka. Joanes de Fontana of Italy designed a surface-running rocket-powered torpedo for setting enemy ships on fire.

By the sixteenth century, however, rockets fell into a time of disuse as weapons of war. But they were still used for fireworks displays, and a German fireworks maker, Johann Schmidlap, invented the step rocket, a multistaged vehicle for lifting fireworks to higher altitudes. Schmidlap's idea is basic to all rockets today that go into outer space.

Nearly all uses of rockets up to this time were for warfare or fireworks, but there is an interesting old Chinese legend that purported to use rockets as a means of transportation. With the help of many assistants, a lesser-known Chinese official named Wan Hu assembled a rocket-powered flying chair. Attached to the chair were two large kites, and fixed to the kites were forty-seven fire-arrow rockets.

On the day of the flight, Wan Hu sat himself on the chair and gave the command to light the rockets. Forty-seven rocket assistants, each armed with torches, rushed forward to light the fuses. In a moment, there was a tremendous roar accompanied by billowing clouds of smoke. When the smoke cleared, Wan Hu and his flying chair were gone. No one knows for sure what happened to Wan Hu, but it is probable that if the event really did take place, Wan Hu and his chair were blown to pieces. Fire-arrows were as apt to explode as to fly.

ROCKETRY BECOMES A SCIENCE

During the latter part of the seventeenth century, the scientific foundations for modern rocketry were laid by the great English scientist Sir Isaac Newton (1642–1727). Newton organized his understanding of physical motion into three scientific laws. These laws explain how rockets work and why they are able to work in the vacuum of outer space. (Newton's three laws of motion will be explained in detail in the next chapter.)

Newton's laws soon began to have a practical impact on the design of rockets. About 1720, a Dutch professor, Willem Gravesande, built model cars propelled by jets of steam. Rocket experimenters in Germany and Russia began working with rockets with a weight of more than 100 pounds (45 kg). Some of these rockets were so powerful that their escaping exhaust flames bore deep holes in the ground even before liftoff.

During the end of the eighteenth century and early into the nineteenth, rockets experienced a brief revival as a weapon of war. The success of Indian rocket barrages against the British in 1792 and again in 1799 caught the interest of an artillery expert, Colonel William Congreve. Congreve set out to design rockets for use by the British military.

The Congreve rockets were highly successful in battle. Used by British ships to pound Fort McHenry in the War of 1812, they inspired Francis Scott Key to write "the rockets' red glare," a line from a poem that later became *The Star Spangled Banner.*

Even with Congreve's work, the accuracy of rockets still had not improved much from the early days. The devastating nature of war rockets was not their accuracy or power, but their numbers. During a typical seige, thousands of them might be fired at the enemy. All over the world, rocket researchers experimented on ways to improve accuracy. An Englishman, William Hale, developed a technique called spin stabilization. In this method, the escaping exhaust gases struck small vanes at the bottom of the rocket, causing it to spin much as a bullet does in flight. Variations of the principle are still used today.

Rockets continued to be used with success in battles all over the European continent. However, in a war with Prussia, the Austrian rocket brigades met their match with newly designed artillery pieces. Breach-loading cannons with rifled barrels and exploding warheads were far more effective weapons of war than the best rockets. Once again, rockets were relegated to peacetime uses.

MODERN ROCKETRY BEGINS

In 1898, a Russian schoolteacher, Konstantin Tsiolkovsky (1857–1935), proposed the idea of space exploration by rocket. In a report he published in 1903, Tsiolkovsky suggested the use of liquid propellants for rockets in order to achieve greater range. Up until then, rocket propellants had always been solid. Tsiolkovsky stated that the speed and range of a rocket were limited only by the exhaust velocity of escaping gases. For his ideas, careful research, and great vision, Tsiolkovsky has been called the father of modern aeronautics.

Early in the twentieth century, an American, Robert H. Goddard (1882–1945), conducted practical experiments in rocketry. He had become interested in a way of achieving higher altitudes than was possible for lighter-than-air balloons. He published a pamphlet in 1919 entitled *A Method of Reaching Extreme Altitudes*. It was a mathematical analysis of what is today called the meteorological sounding rocket.

In his pamphlet, Goddard reached several conclusions important to rocketry. From his tests, he stated that a rocket operates with greater efficiency in a vacuum than in air. At the time, most people mistakenly believed that air was needed for a rocket to push against. Goddard also stated that multistage, or step, rockets were the answer to achieving high altitudes and that the velocity needed to escape the earth's gravity could be achieved in this way.

Goddard's earliest experiments were with solid-propellant rockets. In 1915, he began to try various types of solid fuels and to measure the exhaust velocities of the burning gases.

While working on solid-propellant rockets, Goddard became convinced that a rocket could be propelled better by liquid fuel. No one had ever built a successful liquid-propellant rocket before. It was a much more difficult task than building solid-propellant rockets. Fuel and oxygen tanks, turbines, and combustion chambers would be needed. In spite of the difficulties, Goddard achieved the first successful flight with a liquid-propellant rocket on March 16, 1926. Fueled by liquid oxygen and gasoline, the rocket flew for only two and a half seconds, climbed 41 feet (12.3 m), and landed 184 feet (55.2 m) away in a cabbage patch. By today's standards, the flight was unimpressive. But like the first powered airplane flight by the Wright brothers in 1903, Goddard's gasoline rocket was the forerunner of a whole new era in rocket flight. Goddard, for his achievements, has been called the father of modern rocketry.

Goddard's experiments in liquid-propellant rockets continued for many years. His rockets became bigger and flew higher. He developed a gyroscope system for flight control and a payload compartment for scientific instruments. Parachute recovery systems were employed to return rockets and instruments safely.

The third great space pioneer, Hermann Oberth (b. 1894) of Germany, published a book in 1923 about rocket travel into outer space. His writings were important. Because of them, many small rocket societies sprang up around the world. In Germany, the formation of one such society, the Verein fur Raumschiffahrt (Society for Space Travel), led to the development of the V-2 rocket, which was used against London during World War II. In 1937, thousands of engineers and scientists, including Oberth, assembled in Peenemunde on the shores of the Baltic Sea. There the most advanced rocket of its time would be built and flown.

The V-2 rocket (in Germany called the A-4) was small by comparison to today's rockets. It achieved its great thrust by burning a mixture of liquid oxygen and alcohol at a rate of about one ton every seven seconds. Once launched, the V-2 was a formidable weapon that could devastate whole city blocks.

Dr. Robert H. Goddard standing beside one version of his liquid-propelled rocket.

Fortunately for London and the Allied forces, the V-2 came too late in the war to change its outcome. Nevertheless, by war's end, German rocket scientists and engineers had already laid plans for advanced missiles capable of spanning the Atlantic Ocean and landing in the United States.

With the fall of Germany, many unused V-2 rockets and components were captured by the Allies. Many German rocket scientists came to the United States. Others went to the Soviet Union.

Both the United States and the Soviet Union realized the potential of rocketry as a military weapon and began a variety of experimental programs. At first, the United States began a program with high-altitude atmospheric sounding rockets, one of Goddard's ideas from many years before. Later, a variety of medium- and long-range intercontinental ballistic missiles were developed. These also became the starting point of the U.S. space program. Missiles such as the Redstone, Atlas, and Titan would eventually launch astronauts into earth orbit.

On October 4, 1957, the world was stunned by the news of an earth-orbiting artificial satellite launched by the Soviet Union. Called *Sputnik I*, the satellite was the first successful

Blast-off of a two-stage Titan II Gemini launch vehicle and the *Gemini 10* spacecraft from Cape Kennedy (now Cape Canaveral) on July 18, 1966. Commander John W. Young and pilot Michael Collins, inside the craft, were on a three-day earth orbital mission.

entry in a race for space between the two superpower nations. Less than a month later, the Soviets followed with the launch of a satellite carrying a dog named Laika on board. Laika survived in space for seven days before being put to sleep because her oxygen would soon run out.

A few months after the first *Sputnik*, the United States followed the Soviet Union with a satellite of its own. *Explorer I* was launched on January 31, 1958. In October of that year, the United States formally organized its space program by creating the National Aeronautics and Space Administration (NASA). NASA became a civilian agency with the goal of peaceful exploration of space for the benefit of all humankind.

Soon, many people and machines were being launched into space. Astronauts orbited the earth and landed on the moon. Robot spacecraft traveled to the planets. Space was suddenly opened up to exploration and technology. Satellites not only investigated our world but helped us to forecast the weather and to communicate instantaneously. To do these things, newer and bigger rockets had to be built.

The newest rocket is NASA's Space Shuttle. The Shuttle is the next logical step in rocketry. No longer will rockets have to be thrown away after only one mission. The Space Shuttle is the world's first reusable space launch vehicle.

Since the earliest days of discovery and experimentation, rockets have evolved from simple gunpowder devices into giant vehicles capable of traveling into outer space. Rockets have opened the universe to direct exploration by humankind.

CHAPTER 2

THE PRINCIPLES OF ROCKETRY

A rocket in its simplest form is a chamber enclosing a gas under pressure. A small opening at one end of the chamber allows the gas to escape, and in so doing provides a thrust that propels the rocket in the opposite direction. A good example of this is a balloon. Air inside a balloon is compressed by the balloon's rubber walls. When the neck is released, air escapes and propels the balloon upward. The balloon's flight is highly erratic because there are no structures to stabilize it.

When we think of rockets, we rarely think of balloons. Instead, our attention is drawn to the giant vehicles that carry satellites into orbit and spacecraft to the moon and planets. Regardless, there is a strong similarity between the two. The only significant difference is the way the pressurized gas is produced. With balloons, the gas is pressurized with lung power, but with rockets, the pressure is produced by burning propellants. With modern rockets, the propellants can either be solid or liquid.

One of the interesting facts about the historical development of rockets is that while rockets and rocket-powered devices have been in use for more than two thousand years, it has been only in the last three hundred years that rocket experimenters have had a scientific basis for understanding how they work.

The science of rocketry really began with the publishing of a book in 1687 by the great English scientist Sir Isaac Newton. His book, entitled *Philosophiae Naturalis Principia Mathematica*, described principles in nature. Today, Newton's work is usually just called the *Principia*.

In the *Principia*, Newton stated three important scientific principles that govern the motion of all objects, whether on earth or in space. Knowing these principles, now called Newton's laws of motion, rocketeers have been able to construct the modern giant rockets of today such as the Saturn V and the Space Shuttle. Here now are Newton's laws of motion:

1. Objects at rest will stay at rest or objects in motion will stay in motion unless acted upon by an unbalanced force.

2. The acceleration of an object is directly proportional to the force exerted on that object and inversely proportional to the mass of that object.

3. For every action there is always an opposite and equal reaction.

As will be explained shortly, all three laws are really simple statements of how things move. But with them, precise determinations of rocket performance can be made.

NEWTON'S FIRST LAW

This law of motion is just an obvious statement of fact, but to know what it means, it is necessary to understand the terms *rest, motion,* and *unbalanced force.*

Rest and motion can be thought of as being opposite to each other. Rest is the state of an object when it is not changing position in relation to its surroundings. If you are sitting still in a chair, you can be said to be at rest. This term, however, is relative. Your chair may actually be one of many seats on a speeding airplane. The important thing to remember here is that you are not moving *in relation to your immediate surroundings*. If rest were defined as a total absence of motion, it would not exist in nature. Even if you were sitting in your chair at home, you would still be moving because your chair is actually sitting on the surface of a spinning planet that is orbiting a star, and the star is moving through a rotating galaxy that is, itself, moving through the universe. While sitting "still," you are, in fact, traveling at a speed of hundreds of miles per second.

Motion is also a relative term. All matter in the universe is moving all the time, but in the first law, motion means changing position in relation to surroundings. A ball is at rest if it is sitting on the ground. The ball is in motion if it is rolling. Then it is changing its position in relation to its surroundings. When you are sitting on a chair in an airplane, you are at rest, but if you get up and walk down the aisle, you are in motion. A rocket blasting off the launch pad changes from a state of rest to a state of motion.

The third term important to understanding this law is unbalanced force. If you hold a ball in your hand and keep it still, the ball is at rest. All the time the ball is held there though, it is being acted upon by forces. The force of gravity is trying to pull the ball downward, while at the same time your hand is pushing against the ball to hold it up. The forces acting on the ball are balanced. Let the ball go, or move your hand upward, and the forces become unbalanced. The ball then changes from a state of rest to a state of motion.

In rocket flight, forces become balanced and unbalanced all the time. A rocket on the launch pad is balanced. The surface of the pad holds the rocket up, and the rocket pushes downward. As the engines are ignited, the thrust from the rocket unbalances the forces, and the rocket travels upward. Later, when the rocket runs out of fuel, it slows down, stops at the highest point of its flight, then falls back to the earth.

Rockets in space also react to forces. A rocket in orbit around the earth is in constant motion, but the forces acting on it are balanced. Gravity is trying to pull the rocket down, while centrifugal force is trying to pull it outward. Centrifugal force is the pull you feel as you stand on a spinning platform. During the rotation of the platform, you are pushed toward the outer rim.

To change a rocket's orbit requires that the forces become unbalanced. To go into a higher orbit, a rocket must travel faster. This is accomplished by firing the engine in the proper direction. To go into a lower orbit or return to the earth, the engine must also be fired, but against the direction in which the rocket is traveling. The engine, in this case, acts as a brake. In both instances, going higher or lower, the forces acting on the rocket must be unbalanced for a change in its motion to be accomplished.

Now that the three major terms of the first law have been explained, it is possible to restate this law. If an object, such as a rocket, is at rest, it takes an unbalanced force to make it move. If the object is already moving, it takes an unbalanced force to stop it or to change its direction or speed.

NEWTON'S THIRD LAW

For the time being, we will skip the second law and go directly to the third. This law states that every action has an equal and opposite reaction. If you have ever stepped off a small boat that has not been properly tied to a pier, you will know exactly what this law means.

A rocket can lift off from a launch pad only when it expels gas out of its engine. The rocket pushes on the gas, and the gas in turn pushes on the rocket. The whole process is very similar to riding a skateboard. Imagine that a skateboard and rider are in a state of rest (not moving). The rider steps off the skateboard. In the third law, the stepping off is called an *action*. The skateboard responds to that action by traveling some distance in the opposite direction. The skateboard's motion is called a *reaction*. When the distances traveled by the rider and the skateboard are compared, it would appear that the skateboard had had a much greater reaction than the action of the rider. This was not the case. The reason the skateboard traveled farther is that it weighed less than the rider.

With rockets, the action is the expelling of gas out of the engine. The reaction is the movement of the rocket in the opposite direction. To enable a rocket to lift off from the launch pad, the action, or thrust, from the engine must be greater than the weight of the rocket. In space, however, even tiny thrusts will cause the rocket to change direction.

One of the most commonly asked questions about rockets is how they can work in space where there is no air for them to push against. The answer to this question comes from the third law. Imagine the skateboard again. On the ground, the only part air plays in the motions of the rider and the skateboard is to slow them down. Moving through the air causes friction, or as scientists call it, drag. The surrounding air actually impedes the action-reaction.

Rockets actually work better in space than they do in air. As the exhaust gas leaves the rocket engine it must push away the surrounding air; this uses up some of the energy of the rocket. In space, the exhaust gases can escape freely.

NEWTON'S SECOND LAW

This law of motion is essentially a statement of a mathematical equation. The three parts of the equation are mass (m), acceleration (a), and force (f). Using letters to symbolize each part, the equation can be written as follows:

$$a = \frac{f}{m}$$

By using simple algebra, we can also write the equation two other ways:

$$m = \frac{f}{a} \text{ and } f = ma$$

The last equation is the one most commonly referred to when talking about Newton's second law. It reads: force equals mass times acceleration.

Force in the equation can be thought of as the thrust of the rocket. Mass is the amount of rocket fuel being burned and converted into gas that expands and then escapes from the rocket. Acceleration is the rate at which the gas escapes. Inside the rocket, the gas does not really move, but as it leaves the engine it picks up speed.

The second law of motion is especially useful when designing efficient rockets. To enable a rocket to climb into low earth orbit or escape the earth's gravitational pull, it is necessary to achieve velocities, or speeds, in excess of 17,500 miles (28,000 km) per hour. This is called "escape velocity." Attaining escape velocity requires the rocket engine to achieve the greatest action force possible in the shortest time. In other words, the engine must burn a large mass of fuel and push the resulting gas out of the engine as rapidly as possible. Ways of doing this will be described in the next chapter.

Newton's second law of motion can be restated in the following way: The greater the mass of rocket fuel burned, and the faster the gas produced can escape the engine, the greater the thrust of the rocket.

To summarize, for a rocket to lift off from a launch pad or for a craft in space to change speed or direction, force must be exerted (first law) to unbalance the present forces at work. The amount of force produced will be determined by the mass of rocket fuel that is burned and how fast the gas escapes the rocket (second law). The reaction, or motion, of the rocket is equal to and in an opposite direction from the action, or thrust, from the engine (third law).

CHAPTER 3

PRACTICAL ROCKETRY

The first rockets ever built, the fire-arrows of the Chinese, were not very reliable. Many just exploded on launching. Others flew on erratic courses and landed in the wrong place. Being a rocketeer in the days of the fire-arrows must have been exciting but also a highly dangerous activity.

Today, rockets are much more reliable. They fly on precise courses and are capable of going fast enough to escape the gravitational pull of the earth. Modern rockets are also more efficient because today we have a firm understanding of the scientific principles behind rocketry. This has led us to develop a wide variety of advanced rocket hardware and to devise new propellants that can be used for longer trips and more efficient takeoffs.

ROCKET ENGINES AND THEIR PROPELLANTS

Most rockets today operate with either solid or liquid propellants. The word "propellant" does not simply mean fuel, as you might think. It means both fuel and oxidizer. The fuel is the chemical the rocket burns, but for burning to take place, an oxidizer (oxygen) must be present. Rockets do not have the luxury that jet planes have. Jet engines draw oxygen into their engines from the surrounding air. Rocket engines, which operate mostly in space, where there is no air, must carry their oxygen with them.

Solid-rocket propellants, which are dry to the touch, contain both the fuel and oxidizer combined together in the chemical itself. Usually the fuel is a mixture of hydrogen compounds and carbon. The oxidizer is made up of oxygen compounds. Liquid propellants, which are often gases that have been chilled until they turn into liquids, are kept in separate containers, one for the fuel and the other for the oxidizer. Then, when the engine fires, the fuel and oxidizer are mixed together in the engine.

A solid-propellant rocket has the simplest form of engine. (See Fig. 1.) It has a nozzle, a case, insulation, propellant, and an igniter. The case of the engine is usually a relatively thin metal that is lined with insulation to keep the propellant from burning through. The propellant itself is packed inside the insulation layer.

Many solid rocket engines feature a hollow core that runs through the propellant. In all cases, only the surface of the propellant burns. Rockets that do not have the hollow core must be ignited at the lower end of the propellants. Burning proceeds gradually from one end of the rocket to the other. However, to get higher thrust, the hollow core is used. This increases the surface of the propellants available for burning. The propellants burn from the inside out at a much higher rate, and the gases produced escape the engine at much higher speeds. This gives a greater thrust. Some propellant cores are star-shaped to increase the burning surface even more. (See Fig. 2.)

To fire the solid propellants, many kinds of igniters can be

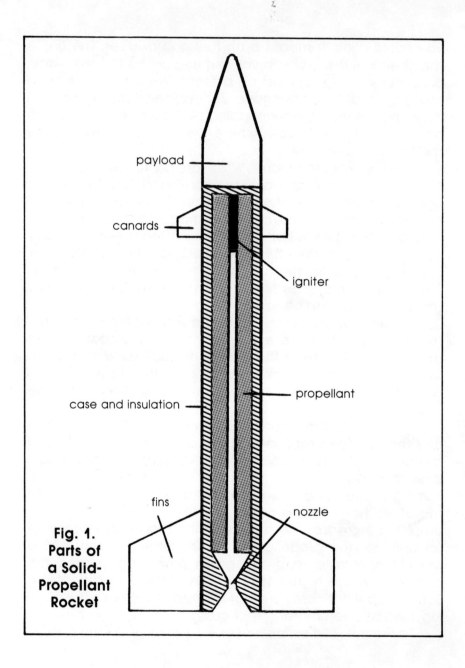

payload

canards

igniter

case and insulation

propellant

fins

nozzle

**Fig. 1.
Parts of
a Solid-
Propellant
Rocket**

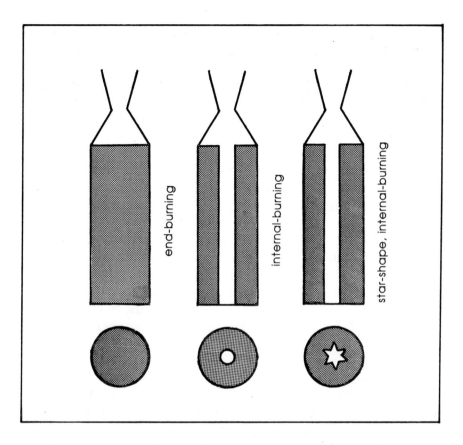

Fig. 2. Different Solid-Propellant Designs

used. Fire arrows were ignited by fuses, but sometimes these ignited too quickly and burned the rocketeer. A far safer and more reliable form of ignition is one that employs electricity. An electric current, coming through wires from some distance away, heats up a special wire inside the rocket. The wire raises the temperature of the propellant it is in contact with to the combustion point.

Many kinds of igniters are more advanced than the hot wire device. Some are encased in a chemical that ignites first, which then ignites the propellants. Other igniters, especially those for large rockets, are rocket engines themselves. The small engine inside the hollow core blasts a stream of flames and hot gas down from the top of the core and ignites the entire surface area of the propellants in a fraction of a second.

The nozzle in a solid-propellant engine is an opening at the back of the rocket that permits the hot expanding gases to escape. The narrow part of the nozzle is the throat. Just beyond the throat is the exit cone. (See Fig. 3.)

The purpose of the nozzle is to increase the acceleration of the gases as they leave the rocket and thereby maximize the thrust. It does this by cutting down the opening through which the gases can escape. To see how this works, you can experiment with a garden hose that has a spray nozzle attachment. This kind of nozzle does not have an exit cone, but that does not matter in the experiment. The important point about the nozzle is that the size of the opening can be varied.

Start with the opening at its widest point. Watch how far the water squirts and feel the thrust produced by the departing water. Now reduce the diameter of the opening, and again note the distance the water squirts and feel the thrust. Rocket nozzles work the same way.

As with the inside of the rocket case, insulation is needed to protect the nozzle from the hot gases. The usual insulation is one that gradually erodes as the gas passes through. Small pieces of the insulation get very hot and break away from the nozzle. As they are blown away, heat is carried away with them.

The other main kind of rocket engine is one that uses liquid propellants. (See Fig. 3.) This is a much more complicated engine, as is evidenced by the fact that solid rocket

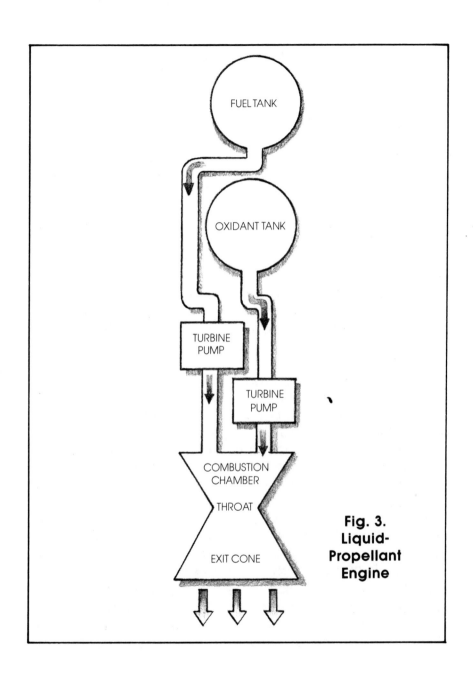

FUEL TANK

OXIDANT TANK

TURBINE
PUMP

TURBINE
PUMP

COMBUSTION
CHAMBER

THROAT

EXIT CONE

Fig. 3.
Liquid-
Propellant
Engine

engines were used for at least seven hundred years before the first successful liquid engine was tested. Liquid propellants have separate storage tanks—one for the fuel and one for the oxidizer. They also have pumps, a combustion chamber, and a nozzle.

The fuel of a liquid engine is usually kerosene or liquid hydrogen; the oxidizer is usually liquid oxygen. They are combined inside a cavity called the *combustion chamber*. Here the propellants burn and build up high temperatures and pressures, and the expanding gas escapes through the nozzle at the lower end. To get the most power from the propellants, they must be mixed as completely as possible. Small nozzles on the roof of the chamber spray and mix the propellants at the same time. Because the chamber operates under high pressures, the propellants need to be forced inside. Powerful, lightweight turbine pumps between the propellant tanks and combustion chambers take care of this job.

With any rocket, and especially with liquid-propellant rockets, weight is an important factor. In general, the heavier the rocket, the more thrust that is needed to get it off the ground. Because of the pumps and fuel lines, liquid engines are much heavier than solid engines.

One especially good method of reducing the weight of liquid engines is to make the exit cone of the nozzle out of very lightweight metals. However, the extremely hot, fast-moving gases that pass through the cone would quickly melt thin metal. Therefore, a cooling system is needed. A highly effective though complex cooling system that is used with some liquid engines takes advantage of the low temperature of liquid hydrogen. Hydrogen becomes a liquid when it is chilled to $-423°F$ ($-253°C$). Before injecting the hydrogen into the combustion chamber, it is first circulated through small tubes that lace the walls of the exit cone. In a cutaway view, the exit cone wall looks like the edge of corrugated cardboard. The hydrogen in the tubes absorbs the excess heat entering the cone walls and prevents it from melting the walls away. It also makes the hydrogen more energetic because of the heat it picks up. We call this kind of cooling system *regenerative cooling*.

ENGINE THRUST CONTROL

Controlling the thrust of an engine is very important to launching payloads (cargoes) into orbit. Too much thrust or thrust at the wrong time can cause a satellite to be placed in the wrong orbit or sent too far out into space to be useful. Too little thrust can cause the satellite to fall back to the earth.

Liquid-propellant engines control the thrust by varying the amount of propellant that enters the combustion chamber. A computer in the rocket's guidance system determines the amount of thrust that is needed and controls the propellant flow rate. On more complicated flights, such as going to the moon, the engines must be started and stopped several times. Liquid engines do this by simply starting or stopping the flow of propellants into the combustion chamber.

Solid-propellant rockets are not as easy to control as liquid rockets. Once started, the propellants burn until they are gone. They are very difficult to stop or slow down part way into the burn. Sometimes, fire extinguishers are built into the engine to stop the rocket in flight. But using them is a tricky procedure and doesn't always work. Some solid-fuel engines have hatches on their sides that can be cut loose by remote control to release the chamber pressure and terminate thrust.

The burn rate of solid propellants is carefully planned in advance. The hollow core running the length of the propellants can be made into a star shape. At first, there is a very large surface available for burning, but as the points of the star burn away, the surface area is reduced. For a time, less of the propellant burns, and this reduces thrust. The Space Shuttle uses this technique to reduce vibrations early in its flight into orbit.

CAUTION: Although most rockets used by governments and research organizations are very reliable, there is still great danger associated with the building and firing of rocket engines. Individuals interested in rocketry should *never* attempt to build their own engines. Even the most simple-looking rocket engines are very complex. Case-wall bursting strength, propellant packing density, nozzle design, and propellant chemistry are all design problems beyond the scope of most amateurs. Many home-built rocket engines have exploded in the faces of their builders with tragic con-sequences. Chapter Five presents an exciting alternative to building rocket engines that allows experimentation in rock-etry but with a high degree of safety.

STABILITY AND CONTROL SYSTEMS

Building an efficient rocket engine is only part of the problem in producing a successful rocket. The rocket must also be stable in flight. A stable rocket is one that flies in a smooth, uniform direction. An unstable rocket flies along an erratic path, sometimes tumbling or changing direction. Unstable rockets are dangerous because it is not possible to predict where they will go. They may even turn upside down and suddenly head back directly to the launch pad.

Making a rocket that is stable requires some form of con-trol system. Controls can be either active or passive. The dif-ference between these and how they work will be explained later. It is first important to understand what makes a rocket stable or unstable.

All matter regardless of size, mass, or shape has a point inside called the *center of mass* (CM). The center of mass is

the exact spot where all of the mass of that object is perfectly balanced. You can easily find the center of mass of an
object such as a ruler by balancing the object on your finger.
If the material used to make the ruler is of uniform thickness
and density, the center of mass should be at the halfway
point between one end of the stick and the other. If the ruler
were made of wood, and a heavy nail were driven into one
of its ends, the center of mass would no longer be in the middle. The balance point would then be nearer the end with
the nail.

The center of mass is important in rocket flight because it
is around this point that an unstable rocket tumbles. As a
matter of fact, any object in flight tends to tumble. Throw a
stick, and it tumbles end over end. Throw a ball, and it spins in
flight. The act of spinning or tumbling is a way of becoming
stabilized in flight. A Frisbee will go where you want it to only if
you throw it with a deliberate spin. Try throwing a Frisbee
without spinning it. If you succeed, you will see that the Frisbee flies in an erratic path and falls far short of its mark.

In flight, spinning or tumbling takes place around one or
more of three axes within the object. These axes are illustrated in Fig. 4. They are called *roll, pitch,* and *yaw.* The point
where all three of these axes intersect is the center of mass.
For rocket flight, the pitch and yaw axes are the most important because any movement in either of these two directions
can cause the rocket to go off course. The roll axis is the least
important because movement along this axis will not affect
the flight path. In fact, a rolling motion will help stabilize the
rocket in the same way a properly passed football is stabilized by rolling (spiraling) it in flight. Although a poorly passed
football may still fly to its mark even if it tumbles rather than
rolls, a rocket will not. The action-reaction energy of a football pass will be completely expended by the thrower the
moment the ball leaves the hand. With rockets, thrust from
the engine is still being produced while the rocket is in flight.
Unstable motions about the pitch and yaw axes will cause

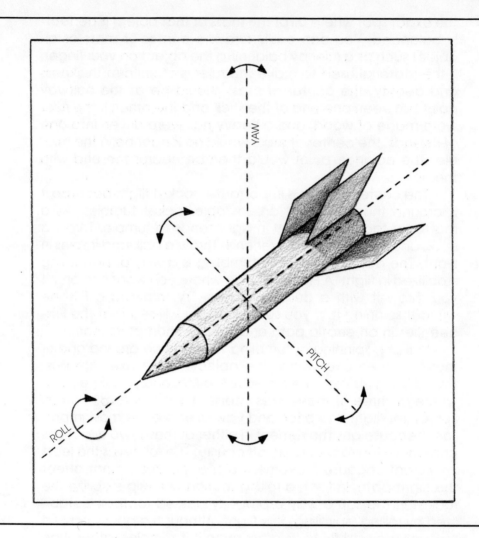

Fig. 4. Roll, Pitch, and Yaw Axes

the rocket to leave the planned course. To prevent this, a control system is needed to prevent or at least minimize unstable motions.

In addition to center of mass, there is another important center inside the rocket that affects its flight. This is the *center of pressure* (CP). The center of pressure exists only when air is flowing past the moving rocket. This flowing air, rubbing and pushing against the outer surface of the rocket, can cause it to begin moving around one of its three axes. Think for a moment of a weather vane. A weather vane is an arrowlike stick that is mounted on a rooftop and is used for telling wind direction. The arrow is attached to a vertical rod that acts as a pivot point. The arrow is balanced so that the center of mass is right at the pivot point. When the wind blows, the arrow turns, and the head of the arrow points into the oncoming wind. The tail of the arrow points in the downwind direction.

The reason that the weather vane arrow points into the wind is that the tail of the arrow has a much larger surface area than the arrowhead. The flowing air imparts a greater force to the tail than the head, and therefore the tail is pushed away. There is a point in the arrow where there is exactly the same surface area on one side of the point as on the other. This spot is called the center of pressure. Note in the diagram shown (Fig. 5) that the center of pressure is not in the same place as the center of mass. If it were, then neither end of the arrow would be favored by the wind and the arrow would not point. The center of pressure is between the center of mass and the tail end of the arrow. This means that the tail end has more surface area than the head end.

It is extremely important that the center of pressure in a rocket be located toward the tail and the center of mass be located toward the nose. If they are in the same place or very near each other, then the rocket will be unstable in flight. The rocket will then try to rotate about the center of mass in the pitch and yaw axes, producing a dangerous situation. With the center of pressure located in the right place, the nose of the rocket will point in the direction of air flow and remain stable.

Control systems for rockets are intended to keep a rocket stable in flight and to steer it. Small rockets usually require only a stabilizing control system, but large rockets, such as the ones that launch satellites into orbit, require a system that not only stabilizes the rocket but also enables it to change course while in flight.

Controls on rockets can either be active or passive. Passive controls are fixed devices that keep rockets stabilized by their very presence on the rocket's exterior. Active controls can be moved while the rocket is in flight to stabilize and steer the craft.

The simplest of all passive controls is a stick. The Chinese fire-arrows were simple rockets mounted on the ends of sticks. The stick kept the center of pressure behind the center of mass. In spite of this, fire-arrows were notoriously inaccurate. Before the center of pressure could take effect, air had to be flowing past the rocket. While still on the ground and immobile, the arrow might lurch and fire the wrong way.

Years later, the accuracy of fire-arrows was improved considerably by mounting them in a trough aimed in the proper direction. The trough guided the arrow in the right direction until it was moving fast enough to be stable on its own.

As will be explained in the next section, the weight of the rocket is a critical factor in performance and range. The fire-arrow sticks added too much dead weight to the rocket, and therefore their range was considerably limited.

An important improvement in rocketry came with the replacement of sticks by clusters of lightweight fins mounted around the lower end near the nozzle. Fins could be made out of lightweight materials and be streamlined in shape.

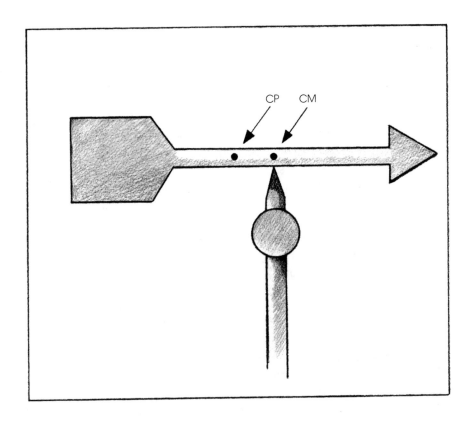

Fig. 5. Weather Vane

They gave rockets a dartlike appearance. The large surface area of the fins easily kept the center of pressure behind the center of mass. Some experimenters even bent the lower tips of the fins in a pinwheel fashion to promote rapid spinning in flight. With these "spin fins," rockets became much more stable in flight. But this design also produces more drag and limits the rocket's range.

With the start of modern rocketry in the twentieth century, new ways were sought to improve rocket stability and at the same time reduce overall rocket weight. The answer to this was the development of active controls. Active control systems included vanes, tilting fins, canards, gimbaled nozzles, vernier rockets, fuel injection, and attitude-control rockets. Tilting fins and canards are quite similar to each other in appearance. (See Fig. 6.) The only real difference between them is their location on the rockets. Canards are mounted on the front end of the rocket while the tilting fins are at the rear. In flight, the fins and canards tilt like rudders to deflect the air flow and cause the rocket to change course. Motion sensors on the rocket detect unplanned directional changes, and corrections can be made by slight tilting of the fins and canards. The advantage of these two devices is size and weight. They are smaller and lighter and produce less drag than the large fins.

Other active control systems can eliminate fins and canards altogether. By tilting the angle at which the exhaust gas leaves the rocket engine, course changes can be made in flight. One of several techniques can be used for changing exhaust direction. (See Fig. 7.)

Vanes are small finlike devices that are placed inside the exhaust of the rocket engine. Tilting the vanes deflects the exhaust, and, by action-reaction, the rocket responds by pointing the opposite way.

Another method for changing the exhaust direction is to gimbal the nozzle. A gimbaled nozzle is one that is able to sway while exhaust gases are passing through it. By tilting the

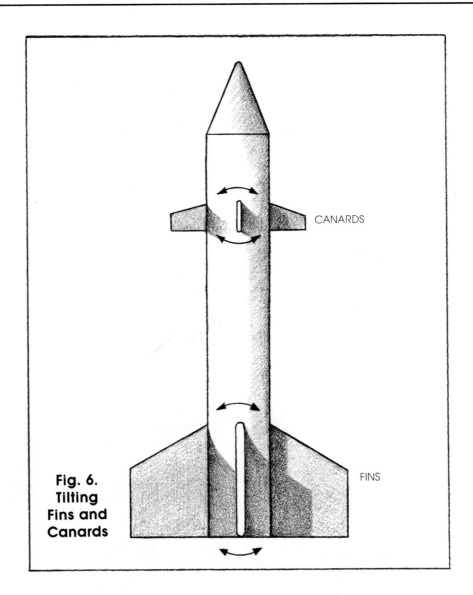

CANARDS

FINS

**Fig. 6.
Tilting
Fins and
Canards**

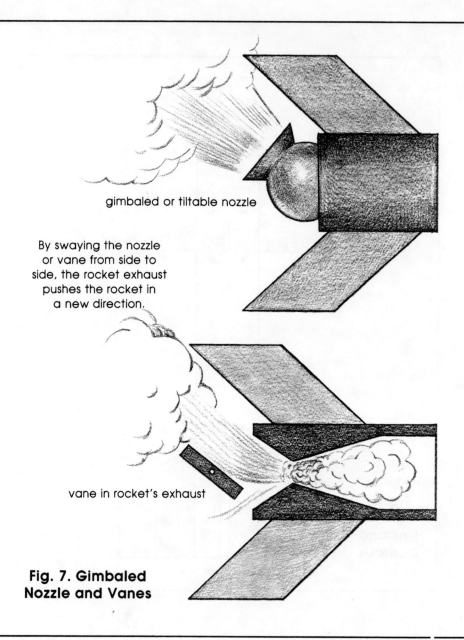

gimbaled or tiltable nozzle

By swaying the nozzle
or vane from side to
side, the rocket exhaust
pushes the rocket in
a new direction.

vane in rocket's exhaust

**Fig. 7. Gimbaled
Nozzle and Vanes**

engine nozzle in the proper direction, the rocket responds by changing course.

Vernier rockets can also be used to change direction. These are small rockets mounted to the outside of the large engine. When needed they fire, producing the desired course change.

In space, only by spinning the rocket along the roll axis or by using active controls involving the engine exhaust can the rocket be stabilized or have its direction changed. Without air, fins and canards have nothing to work upon. (Science fiction movies showing rockets in space with wings and fins are long on fiction and short on science.) The most common kinds of active control used in space are attitude-control rockets. (See Fig. 8.) Small clusters of engines are mounted all around the vehicle. By firing the right combination of these small rockets, the vehicle can be turned in any direction. As soon as they are aimed properly, the main engines fire, sending the rocket off in the new direction.

WEIGHT

There is another important factor affecting the performance of a rocket. The weight of a rocket can make the difference between a successful flight and just wallowing around on the launch pad. As a basic principle of rocket flight, it can be said that for a rocket to leave the ground, the engine must produce a thrust that is greater than the total weight of the vehicle. It is obvious that a rocket with a lot of unnecessary weight will not be as efficient as one that is trimmed to just the bare essentials.

For an ideal rocket, the total weight of the vehicle should be distributed along the following general formula: Of the total mass, 91 percent should be propellants; 3 percent should be tanks, engines, fins, etc.; and 6 percent can be the payload. Payloads may be satellites, astronauts, or spacecraft to other planets or moons.

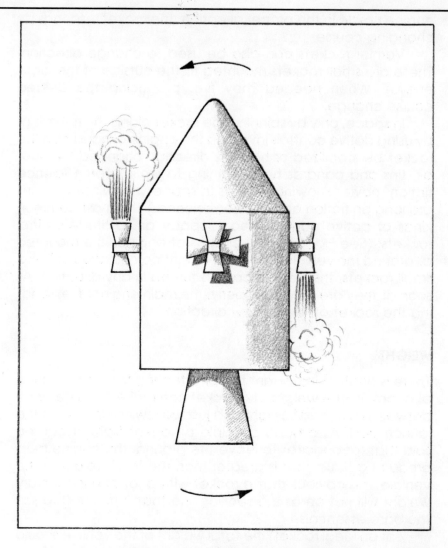

**Fig. 8. Attitude-Control Rockets Changing
a Spacecraft's Direction in Space**

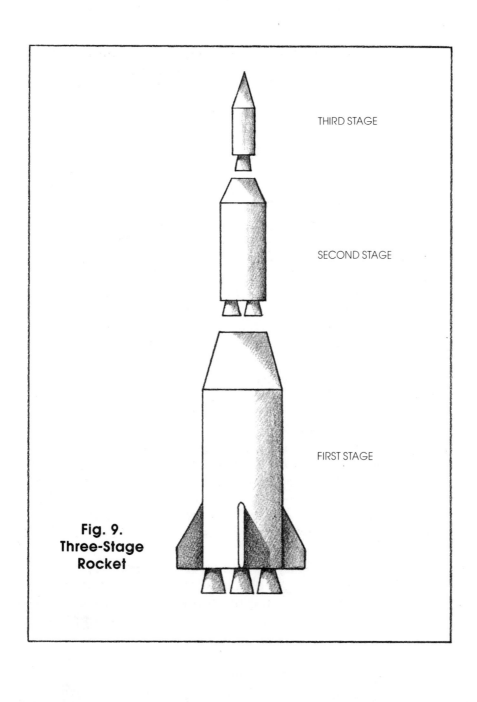

THIRD STAGE

SECOND STAGE

FIRST STAGE

**Fig. 9.
Three-Stage
Rocket**

In determining the effectiveness of a rocket design, rocketeers speak in terms of mass fraction (MF). The mass of the propellants of the rocket divided by the total mass of the rocket gives mass fraction:

$$MF = \frac{\text{mass of propellants}}{\text{total mass}}$$

The mass fraction of the ideal rocket given above is 0.91. From the mass fraction formula one might think that an MF of 1.0 is perfect, but then the entire rocket would be nothing more than a lump of propellants that would simply ignite into a fireball. The larger the MF number, the less payload the rocket can carry; the smaller the MF number, the less its range becomes. An MF number of 0.91 is a good balance between payload-carrying capability and range.

Large rockets, able to carry spacecraft into space, have serious weight problems. To reach space and proper orbital velocities, a great deal of propellant is needed, and therefore the tanks, engines, and associated hardware become larger. Up to a point, bigger rockets fly farther than smaller rockets, but when they become too large their structures weigh them down too much, and the mass fraction is reduced to an impossible number.

A solution to the problem of giant rockets weighing too much can be credited to the sixteenth-century fireworks maker Johann Schmidlap. Schmidlap attached small rockets to the top of big ones. When the large rocket was exhausted, the rocket casing was dropped behind and the remaining rocket fired. Much higher altitudes were achieved by this method.

The rockets used by Schmidlap were called step rockets. Today this technique of building rockets is called *staging*. (See Fig. 9.) Thanks to staging, it has become possible not only to reach outer space but the moon and other planets, too.

CHAPTER 4

ROCKETRY
EXPERIMENTS

Most rockets in use today need to burn fuel in order to produce thrust, yet there are many experiments for learning about rocketry that can be conducted without the use of explosive compounds. You probably have many materials and scraps around your house that can be put to good use in experiments. String, wood, soda straws, paper, rubber bands, old cans, and a variety of other household items plus a few inexpensive materials from the store can help you become a rocket expert.

In the next several pages, you will find instructions for conducting experiments that will help you understand rocket principles and the practical aspects of modern rocketry. When conducting any of the following experiments, keep a notebook handy to write your observations in. You may find that some of these experiments make excellent science fair projects.

SPINNING CAN

Materials:

Soup or coffee can	String
Nail	Water
Block of wood	Bucket
Hammer	

Procedure:

1. Using the nail punch three or four holes around the top rim of the can. Use the wood block for support as you hammer the nail through the metal. Be careful in handling the cans; the holes will have sharp edges.

2. Punch four equally spaced holes around the bottom rim of the can.

3. Reinsert the nail into each of the holes, and bend the holes to the side. Make sure each hole is bent in the same direction—clockwise or counterclockwise.

4. Tie pieces of string to the upper rim of the can through the holes punched there. Join the strings together with another string so that the can resembles a hanging planter.

5. Fill the bucket with water, and dip the can in the water until it is full. Lift the can by the string and observe the spinning. (It might be best to do this part outdoors.)

The can spins because of the action-reaction principle of Newton's third law. Each stream of water produces a rotational thrust similar to the way the *Apollo* spacecraft in orbit was rotated with four clusters of attitude-control rockets.

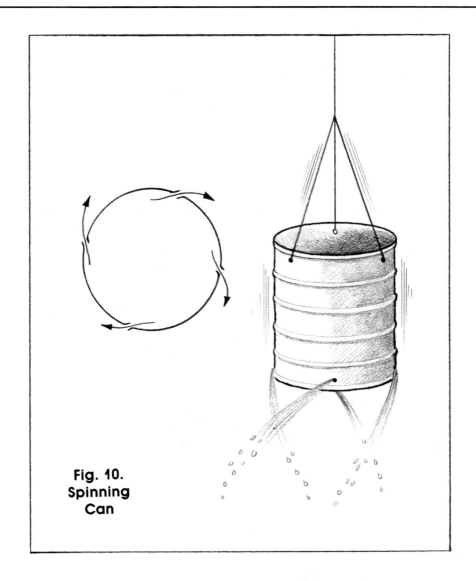

**Fig. 10.
Spinning
Can**

PAPER ROCKETS

Materials:

Paper	Plastic milkshake straw
Fat pencil	(not a paper straw)
Scissors	Cellophane tape

Procedure:

1.Cut a narrow strip of paper and roll it around the pencil. Tape the paper together to form a tube.

2.Cut one end of the tube that you just formed and shape it into a cone. Tape it so that it holds this shape. Be sure not to leave any holes.

Fig. 11. Paper Rockets

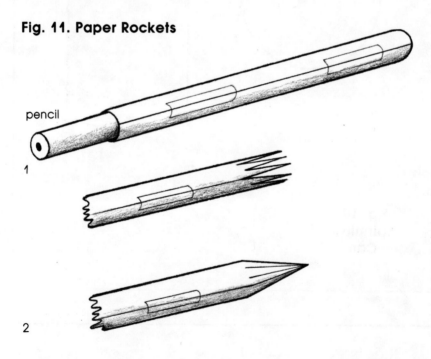

pencil

1

2

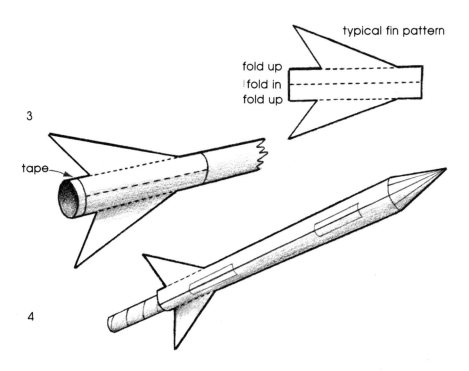

typical fin pattern

fold up
fold in
fold up

3

tape

4

3.Tape fins to the other end of the tube. Experiment with different fin designs.

4.Remove the pencil and insert the straw. Blow sharply through the straw to launch the rocket.

Paper rockets simulate the flight of larger rockets. The fins stabilize your paper rocket. For variety, the tips of the fins can be bent in a pinwheel fashion to produce spinning in flight. Larger winglike fins can be added for gliding flights.

As you build paper rockets, try to use as little tape as possible. The rockets must be sealed so that air from the straw will escape only by pushing the straw forward. Too much tape, however, will add extra weight to the rocket and reduce its range.

ROCKET STAGING

Materials:

2 long balloons
1 paper or styrofoam cup
1 plastic straw cut into four equal lengths
Masking tape
30 to 65 feet (about 10 to 20 m) of heavy thread
     or braided nylon (not monofilament) fishing line

Procedure:

1.Cut out the bottom of the cup.

2.Slide the four pieces of straw onto the line and tie the ends of the line to supports.

3.Place one balloon inside the open bottom of the cup and inflate it.

4.While holding on to the neck of the inflated balloon, insert the end of the second balloon and inflate this balloon also. When the second balloon expands into the cup, the nozzle of the first balloon should be squeezed shut.

5.Tape the balloons to the straws as shown in the diagram. You may need an assistant for this part.

6.When all is ready, launch your two-stage rocket by releasing the nozzle of the second balloon. When the balloon you are holding is finished thrusting, the first balloon (second stage) will automatically "fire" and travel farther along the string.

7.Use your ingenuity and try other arrangements for the balloons such as side by side.

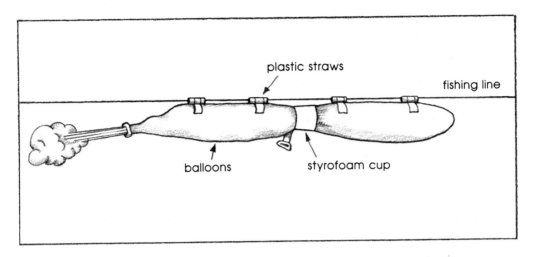

Fig. 12. Rocket Staging

With large launch vehicles, intended to travel into space, the weight of the engines and propellant tanks becomes a critical factor. By constructing the rocket in smaller stages, tanks and engines can be discarded as the propellants are used up. This greatly reduces vehicle weight and makes the remaining stages more efficient.

"POP" BOTTLE

Materials:

Glass bottle with narrow neck
Rubber stopper that fits the neck
    (try a chemical supply store
    or ask to borrow one from
    a school science laboratory)
Baking soda
Vinegar
Tissue paper
Short lengths of dowel rods or several round pencils

Procedure:

1.Place a small amount of water and a few tablespoons of vinegar inside the bottle.

2.Wrap two tablespoons of baking soda in a few layers of tissue paper.

3.Lay the dowel rods in a straight row along a tabletop.

4.Drop the wrapped baking soda into the water and cork the bottle. Make sure the cork makes a snug fit, but do not ram it into the bottle.

5.Lay the bottle on the dowel rods and stand to the side. Be prepared to clean up any water that is spilled from the bottle.

The pop bottle moves because of the action-reaction generated by the popping of the cork.

    When the vinegar and water soak through the tissue to the baking soda, bubbling begins. Pressure builds up inside the bottle and finally pops the stopper. The bottle rolls away in the opposite direction due to action-reaction. In this

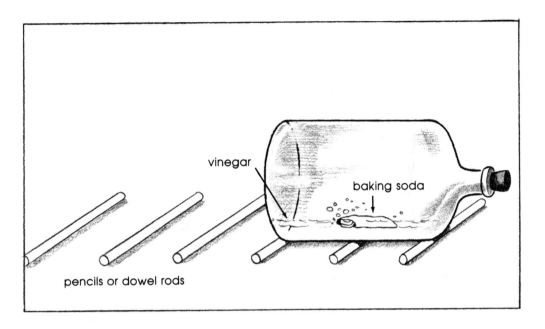

vinegar

baking soda

pencils or dowel rods

Fig. 13. "Pop" Bottle

experiment, you may have to try different amounts of water, vinegar, and baking soda to get the greatest reaction on the bottle. A test tube can be substituted for the bottle if you have one, but then use smaller quantities of the ingredients.

CO$_2$ ROCKET

Materials:

CO$_2$ (carbon dioxide) cartridge
    (available at hobby shops)
Puncture tool for CO$_2$ cartridge
    (also available at hobby shops)
Plastic soda straw
Braided nylon fishing line
    (not heavy thread or monofilament fishing line)
Masking tape
Heavy paper (the back of a paper pad will do)
Foam rubber pad

Procedure:

1.Roll a tube from the heavy paper and fasten it together with tape. The tube should be just large enough to hold the CO$_2$ cartridge.

2.Make a cone from the heavy paper and tape it to one end of the tube.

3.Insert the CO$_2$ cartridge into the tube so that half of it sticks out—the nozzle end. Wrap the tube and cartridge with enough tape so that it cannot slip.

4.Slide a few short pieces of soda straw over the fishing line and tie the ends of the line between two trees outside that are about 50 feet (15 m) apart.

5.Firmly tape the tube to the straws.

6.Protect the far end of the fishing line support with the foam pad.

7.Clear the area of spectators around the far end of the fishing line, and when ready fire the CO$_2$ cartridge with the puncture tool.

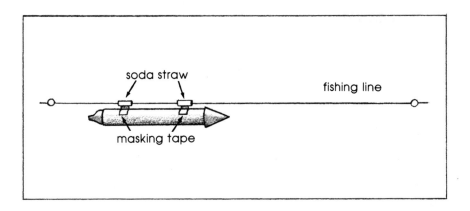

Fig. 14. CO$_2$ Rocket

CAUTION: This rocket will move very fast, and since it is a metal projectile could seriously injure anyone it hits. Do this experiment outdoors only. Also, throw away the expended CO$_2$ cartridge. Reloading old CO$_2$ cartridges and trying to light them with matches is extremely dangerous.

This experiment demonstrates Newton's third law of motion by the action-reaction of the CO$_2$ cartridge. From the results of the water rocket and Newton car experiments coming up, one might anticipate that the CO$_2$ rocket would not travel very fast. The only propellant inside the cartridge is a compressed gas—CO$_2$, or carbon dioxide. The reason why the rocket does travel fast is that the gas is so compressed that when it escapes it has an extremely high acceleration. This makes up for the low mass of the gas.

WATER ROCKET

Materials:

Water rocket (available in toy stores)
Water

Procedure:

This experiment should be done outdoors only.

1.Assemble the rocket and pump as shown in the diagram included in the manufacturer's package.

2.Pump the rocket twenty times but do not add any water to its case. Fire the rocket and estimate how high it climbed. You may want to have an assistant standing a short distance away to estimate and note down the rocket's altitude—how high it traveled on this first flight.

3.Now add a small amount of water to the rocket case, and again pump it twenty times. Fire the rocket and estimate how high it climbed. Again note how high it traveled.

4.Try different amounts of water and different amounts of pumping, and each time determine how high the rocket climbed.

Water rockets work by releasing air pressure from inside their cases. Water, also inside the case, is forced out the nozzle, and the combination of escaping water and air produces a thrust that propels the rocket upward. This experiment, like the others, illustrates Newton's third law of motion—action-reaction.

By firing the water rocket with different amounts of water and air, Newton's second law of motion is also illustrated. In the second law, the force or thrust is equal to mass times acceleration. Compressed air inside the case provides the

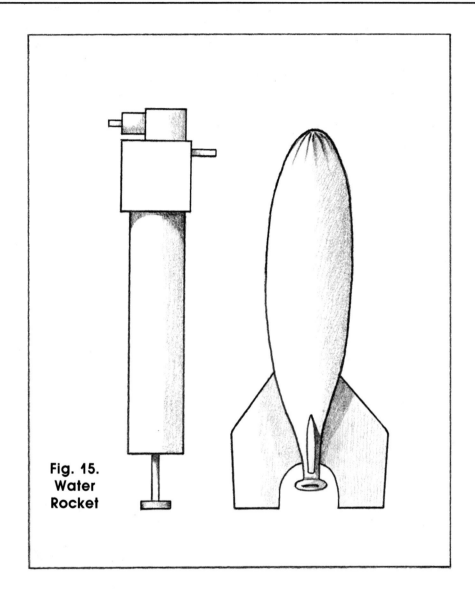

Fig. 15.
Water
Rocket

acceleration and water provides the mass. From your experiment, you should have observed that the rocket did not climb very high when it had only air inside. The air by itself has little mass and therefore does not produce much thrust on its own. If you tried to fly the rocket with all water and no air, you would see that it didn't travel upward at all. The water has a large mass, but by dribbling out of the nozzle, it has almost no acceleration. The best flights come when both mass and acceleration are large.

NEWTON CAR

Materials:

Blocks of wood
Three large nails
Drill
Ten round pencils or short
    lengths of dowel rods
String
Rubber bands
Lead fishing sinkers
Matches

Procedure:

1.Cut and shape the wood blocks to resemble the blocks in the picture. Hammer the three nails into one of the blocks in the position shown.

2.Drill three holes in the second block so that the lead sinkers can be inserted when needed.

3.Tie twelve small loops of string. Make them all exactly the same size.

4.Slip one of the string loops over one rubber band. Stretch the rubber band over the two nails at the front of the first block. Pull the string back and slip it over the third nail. The device should now look something like a slingshot.

5.Carefully arrange all the pencils or dowel rods in one long row. Place each pencil or rod exactly 2 inches (5 cm) apart.

6.Set the Newton car on some of the pencils as shown in the diagram. Insert between the rubber bands the block with the holes.

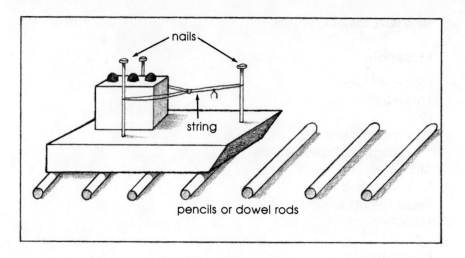

Fig. 16. Newton Car

7. With an adult present, strike a match and carefully set the string on fire. When the string burns through, the slingshot will fire and the Newton car will begin moving.

8. Measure how far the car travels. Make a note of its distance.

9. Set up the car for three more runs, but for the first one add one sinker to the holes. Measure how far the car travels. Add two sinkers for the next run and three for the third.

10. Prepare the car for four more runs, but this time use two rubber bands. Repeat with the three sinkers.

11. Prepare one last set of four runs for the car. This time use three rubber bands.

12. Take all the measurements for the twelve runs of the car and draw a graph that shows the effect of having one, two, and three rubber bands and none, one, two, and three sinkers.

The Newton car experiment is an excellent way to illustrate Newton's action-reaction principle and his second law, which states force equals mass times acceleration. In the second law, the rubber bands represent acceleration and the weight of the block represents mass. The force that results from the action-reaction of throwing the block off the car is measured by the distance the car travels.

CHAPTER 5

MODEL ROCKETRY

In the late 1950s, when the space race was just getting under way, many people, youngsters and adults alike, began experimenting with rocketry. It was natural that the space attempts of the two leading nations in space research, the United States and the Soviet Union, would motivate individuals to imitate, on a small scale, the activities of professional rocket scientists. Unfortunately, many of these amateur experiments ended in disaster.

While the scientific principles governing rockets may be simple to understand, the technical problems in producing a successful and safe rocket motor are enormous. Some amateur experimenters were killed when their rockets exploded, sometimes while still in their hands. Others lost eyes, fingers, hands, or were disfigured as a result of the blasts. Some of the mishaps even took place while students were being supervised by teachers. Amateur rocketry rapidly became a national problem in the United States. There was a public cry for laws to outlaw amateur rocket experiments.

Then came a solution to the problem. Although interest in rocketry sometimes led to injuries, the interest itself was actually a good thing. Future scientists could be expected from the ranks of juvenile experimenters. The solution was not to stop rocket experiments, but to make them safe.

Model manufacturers began to work on designing and producing safe rocket engines. These would have to have excellent performance characteristics yet be safe and economical at the same time.

Soon, a new engine was produced that was so safe it could be shipped through the mail. With this new engine, the hobby and sport of model rocketry was born. Model rocketeers, rather than experiment with building engines, could devote their entire time to designing the external parts of the rocket. Payloads, staging, recovery, and high altitudes then became the absorbing interest. The new rockets could be built with materials such as paper, balsa wood, and plastic.

MODEL ROCKET ENGINES

The new rocket engine consisted of a heavy paper cylinder or case that held a charge of gunpowder. On one end of the case was a nozzle of compressed clay and on the other end a paper cap. (See Fig. 17.) By use of an electric igniter, the propellant burned and produced a brief but considerable thrust over a period of a few seconds. A small charge of smoke-producing powder burned after the propellant, producing a visible streak in the sky. Finally, a small ejection charge fired, activating the rocket's recovery system.

The trick in making the engine was to compress the propellant to the exact amount to allow it to burn quickly but not explode. If an explosion were to occur, the nozzle would be harmlessly blasted out of the bottom and the paper cap out of the top at the same time. The paper case, however, is left safely intact. With home-built engines, the case usually

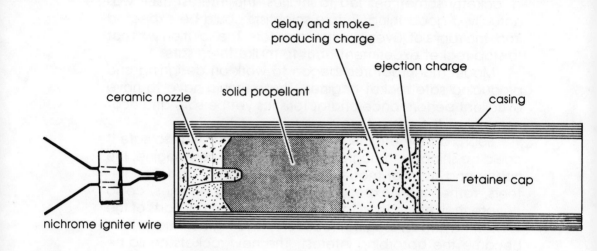

delay and smoke-producing charge

ejection charge

ceramic nozzle

solid propellant

casing

nichrome igniter wire

retainer cap

Fig. 17. Model Rocket Engine

bursts, spraying the experimenters with dangerous metal shrapnel.

One of the important features of model rocket engines is that they are designed to slip in and out of the body of the rocket. Unlike most rockets designed by scientists for use in launching satellites, model rockets are reusable. After a launch, the rocket engine is replaced with a new engine for the next flight.

Since the first model rocket engines were developed, many new engines have been produced featuring different sizes, thrusts, and burning times. Model rocketeers are now presented with many options for powering their rockets.

—62—

Some of the engines available are even capable of accelerating a model rocket to supersonic speed.

The smallest and least expensive of the model engines available are the mini-engines. These engines have a length of 1.75 inches (4.45 cm) and a diameter of 0.5 inches (1.27 cm). The next largest engines are the standard A, B, and C engines, which all have a length of 2.75 inches (6.69 cm) and a diameter of 0.7 inches (1.75 cm). The largest engine available from most major rocket manufacturers is the D engine, which has a length of 2.75 inches (6.99 cm) and a diameter of 0.96 inches (2.4 cm). Larger engines—sizes E and F, for example—are available and are widely used but require very large launching ranges for safe use. Beginners in rocketry should try to master model rocketry with the mini- or standard engines before graduating to the D, E, or F engines.

On the paper case of each engine is a code that gives information about the engine's expected performance. The first symbol, a letter, indicates the total power of the engine. B engines are twice as powerful as A engines, C engines are twice as powerful as B engines, and so on. The number that follows the letter gives the average thrust rounded off to the nearest newton. A newton is the metric unit for thrust. Approximately 4.45 newtons equal a pound (0.45 kg) of thrust. The third number indicates the time in seconds between when the propellants are used up and the ejection charge fires.

Special engines are available to serve as booster stages for multiple stage rockets. These engines do not have a time delay. As soon as the propellants for the booster engine are exhausted, hot gases shoot up into the nozzle of an engine directly above and ignite its propellants.

THE BODY OF THE ROCKET

Rockets that hold the rolled paper and gunpowder engines are constructed out of paper, balsa wood, plastic, rubber,

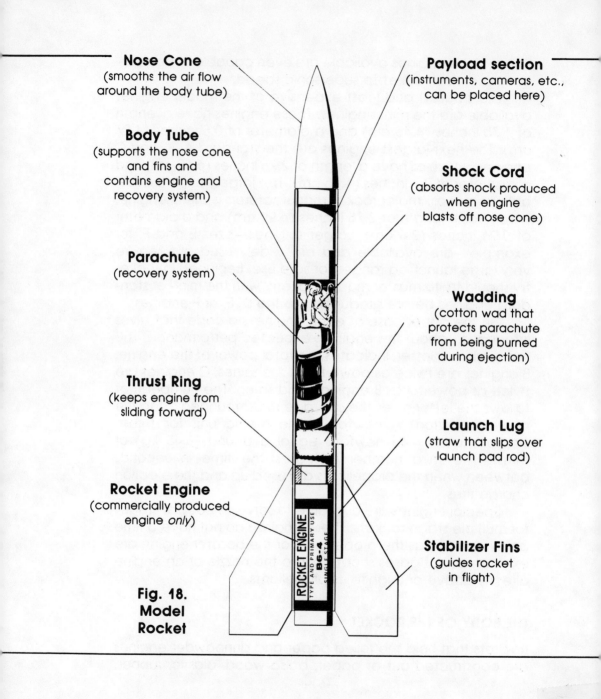

Nose Cone
(smooths the air flow
around the body tube)

Body Tube
(supports the nose cone
and fins and
contains engine and
recovery system)

Parachute
(recovery system)

Thrust Ring
(keeps engine from
sliding forward)

Rocket Engine
(commercially produced
engine *only*)

**Fig. 18.
Model
Rocket**

Payload section
(instruments, cameras, etc.,
can be placed here)

Shock Cord
(absorbs shock produced
when engine
blasts off nose cone)

Wadding
(cotton wad that
protects parachute
from being burned
during ejection)

Launch Lug
(straw that slips over
launch pad rod)

Stabilizer Fins
(guides rocket
in flight)

ROCKET ENGINE
TYPE AND PRIMARY USE
B6-4
SINGLE STAGE

glue, and paint. (See Fig. 18.) The body of the rocket is a tube made of paper. Fins fashioned from balsa wood are glued to the lower end of the tube, and a nose cone, usually made of balsa wood or plastic, is inserted in the upper end. Along the side of the body is a short length of soda straw called the launch lug. When the rocket is erect on the launch pad, the launch lug slips over a long, straight rod that is aimed in the proper direction. During the first few moments of flight, the rocket is guided by the rod until it is traveling fast enough for the fins to stabilize its flight.

A few seconds after liftoff, when the rocket is already some distance off the ground, the engine propellant is used up. The smoke-producing powder leaves a streak of smoke in the sky and makes following the rocket easy. At the proper moment, the explosive ejection charge fires, and this triggers the rocket's recovery system. Usually, the rocket is designed to separate just below the nose cone, and a parachute from within the body pops out. The vehicle can then safely return to the ground for another flight.

HOW TO BEGIN

To participate in model rocketry, you will need to obtain the following: a model rocket, engines, a launch pad, and a launch control system. All of these items are available from hobby shops or mail-order catalogs of hobby stores and come in a wide variety of styles. Depending upon the particular equipment chosen, a complete setup can be purchased for under $20. Some items, such as the launch pad and control system, can probably be assembled from scraps and supplies you already have at home and thereby save a large share of the setup cost. Plans for home-built launch pads and control systems will be found near the end of this chapter. The only thing you should never attempt to construct yourself is the rocket engine.

It is best when beginning in model rocketry to purchase a complete rocket kit. Rockets from kits have been flight tested. If you construct them properly, they should perform well and safely. With the kit, you will find all the information you need to assemble the rocket and fly it. As you become more experienced in model rocketry, however, you will find that the real enjoyment and excitement comes not from putting together a kit but from designing your own rockets and making them do exactly what you have planned. But whether you build rockets from kits or design them yourself, the information that follows will lead you toward becoming a real rocket expert.

ROCKET DESIGN

Commercial manufacturers have produced hundreds of different model rocket kits. Some are needlelike high performance vehicles. Some feature large payload compartments. Others offer unusual recovery systems, multiple stages, or copy spaceships from popular movies such as *Star Wars*. Hobbyists, on their own, have produced thousands of designs. With the exception of three important design-limiting factors, there are a multitude of design possibilities available for model rockets. These three factors are stability, weight, and drag.

Stability

A rocket that shoots straight up into the air is said to be stable. One that tumbles in flight or follows an erratic path is unstable. Dangerous might be a better word than unstable. While tumbling, an unstable rocket might suddenly turn and head straight back for the launch pad at high speed. (See Fig. 19.)

The two important points affecting the stability of a

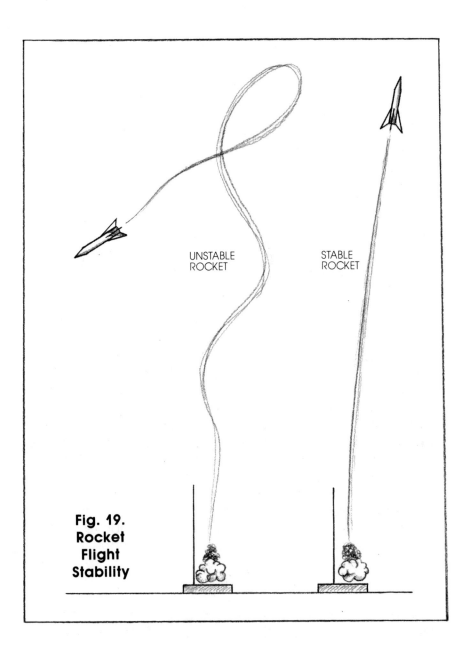

UNSTABLE
ROCKET

STABLE
ROCKET

Fig. 19.
Rocket
Flight
Stability

model rocket are the center of mass and center of pressure. Both of these points have been described in detail earlier. In review, the center of mass, or CM, is a point within a rocket where all the mass of the rocket seems to be concentrated. In other words, the center of mass is its balance point. It is around this point that an unstable rocket tumbles. The center of pressure, or CP, is the point in the rocket that divides the surface area exactly in half.

For a rocket to be stable, the center of pressure must be located behind the center of mass or on the engine end of the rocket. With more surface area located behind the center of mass than in front, the tail end of the rocket always points away from the air streaming around the rocket as it travels through the air. The nose end of the rocket always points into the stream. In flight, rockets work like weather vanes.

A good rule of safety when designing a rocket or assembling a rocket from a kit is that the center of pressure should be at least one body diameter behind the center of mass. Determining where each of these points is located is a relatively easy thing to do and should be done as a safety check before any new rocket, including a rocket from a kit, is flown. To find the center of pressure, a simple diagram of a side view of the rocket should be made on heavy paper, such as on the back of a notebook pad. Great care should be taken to see that the diagram is drawn as accurately as possible. Cut out the diagram and balance it on the edge of a knife. When the balance is found, the center of pressure will be located at the middle of the cutout directly above the knife edge. Mark the cutout with the following symbol:

The center of mass is found in a similar manner. This time, take the assembled rocket and slip a loop of string around it. The rocket should be loaded with the largest engine you are likely to use inside it, and the parachute or other recovery system should be packed inside. The rocket should be prepared just as though you were about to launch it. Slide the string loop until the rocket balances. Place a small piece of tape on the string to keep it from slipping. Now mark the center of mass along the rocket body with a marker that is not permanent. Use the following symbol for center of mass:

To determine if the rocket will be stable, transfer the center of pressure mark from the cutout to the proper place on the rocket model. If the center of pressure is behind the center of mass, the rocket will be stable. Double-check your measurements by carefully swinging the model around you with the string. Let the string out 6 to 8 feet (a few meters) as it is swinging. If the rocket tumbles while circling you, it is not stable. If it travels around in a smooth path, or at least corrects itself as the speed picks up, the rocket will be stable.

Rockets that are unstable can be made stable in a relatively easy manner. A small amount of weight in the form of a lump of clay placed in the rocket's nose will shift the center of mass forward and stabilize the rocket. If a large amount of clay is needed, it might be better to modify the rocket design. Any additional weight added to the rocket reduces the altitude it can reach. Increasing the size of the fins slightly might solve the stability problem by moving the center of pressure back. It is important, however, not to make the fins too large. If the rocket is flown on a windy day, strong crosswinds could cause your rocket to veer sideways and fly into the wind. Large fins promote rapid corrections when the air stream changes. The correction effect is called "weathercocking," and rockets with large fins are often lost when they travel far astray from the launch site.

Weight

The height a model rocket will reach is determined by three things. First, the size of the engine will affect the altitude the rocket reaches. The more powerful the engine, the higher the rocket will climb. The amount of drag, or air resistance, the external shape of the rocket produces in flight will also affect its altitude. Drag will be described in the next section. The last factor affecting the rocket's altitude is its weight. A lightweight rocket will fly higher than a heavy rocket.

To increase a rocket's altitude, the lightest possible construction materials for the rocket should be chosen. Balsa wood, very thin plywood, or plastic is used for the fins, and balsa wood or plastic is used for the nose cone. Body tubes are usually made out of paper.

When designing a rocket, great care should be taken to choose materials that are strong enough to survive the flight, but, at the same time, are light in weight. While designing the rocket, it is tempting to add large fins, pods, and other structures for styling. These can make the rocket very interesting to fly and display, but remember that any unnecessary structure adds weight to the vehicle, and this subtracts from the altitude it can reach.

Drag

Drag, or resistance to the air, is a major thief of a model rocket's potential altitude. When the rocket is moving, friction with the air slows the vehicle. Any part of the rocket that sticks out contributes to drag. When seen from above, rockets with the smallest cross-section area generally have the least amount of drag. Not only is area important, but the shape of that area and its surface texture are also important to the rocket's performance.

To reduce friction, a rocket should be designed to slice cleanly through the air. A properly designed rocket is said to be streamlined. This means that as air passes around the outside of an object, it flows in nice, smooth lines. Poorly

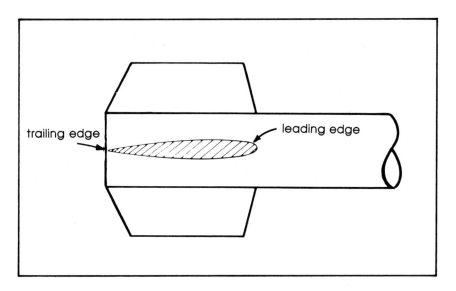

trailing edge

leading edge

Fig. 20. Cross Section View of Streamlined Fin

designed rockets, ones that produce drag, cause the air to tumble. The proper term for tumbling air is *turbulence*.

When designing a rocket or buying a kit, it is valuable for you to decide in advance whether or not high altitude is important to you. Many rocket kits and designs, especially scale models of large launch vehicles and science fiction rockets, feature extra fins, pods, and antennas that make them fun to build and fly but limit their altitude. These models are not usually well streamlined and are heavier than high-altitude models. If altitude is important to you, choose a model that has a small cross section and small fins.

When building any rocket, be sure to improve its stream-line characteristics by sanding smooth all surfaces and shap-ing the leading and trailing edges of the fins as shown in Fig. 20. Paint the model with model enamels to make the surface smoother still. Although paint will add weight to the rocket, it will greatly reduce skin friction with the air. Painting is a valuable trade-off in model rocketry. The effect of the increased weight on altitude is more than offset by reduced drag.

Before painting, seal all balsa wood surfaces with a model paint sealer or with a thin layer of white glue. Balsa wood tends to soak up paint, and the sealer eliminates any unnecessary paint coats.

Plastic rocket parts do not need to be painted. However, there will be some rough edges left over from the molding process, and these should be smoothed with a razor blade or a light sanding.

LAUNCH PADS

The function of a launch pad is twofold. First, it provides a stable platform for assembling the rocket and getting it ready for launch. Second, it guides the rocket for the first few moments after engine ignition until the fins stabilize the rocket's flight.

While there are several good launch pads available for purchase from model rocket supply companies, they are easy to make, and many rocketeers and rocket clubs choose to make their own. All that is needed to make a basic pad are some scraps of wood and metal and the right tools.

A launch pad can be as simple as a large block of wood with a long metal rod sticking straight up from it and a metal blast deflector to prevent the wood from burning. (See Fig. 21.) Rods can be made out of straightened coat hangers, but unless you can make it perfectly straight, it is best to buy a rod from a hardware store or hobby shop. Welding rods are suitable. The rod should be about 30 inches (75 cm) long and just small enough so that the launch lugs of a rocket can slip over it. Be careful not to let the rod become bent; any bends will produce friction on the launch lug and steal some of the rocket's altitude. Blast deflectors can easily be made out of

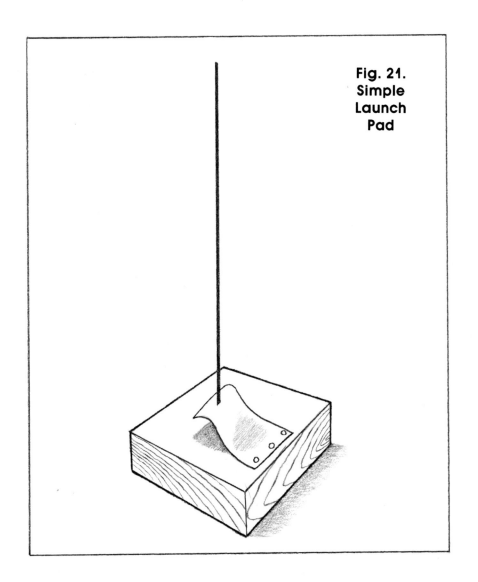

**Fig. 21.
Simple
Launch
Pad**

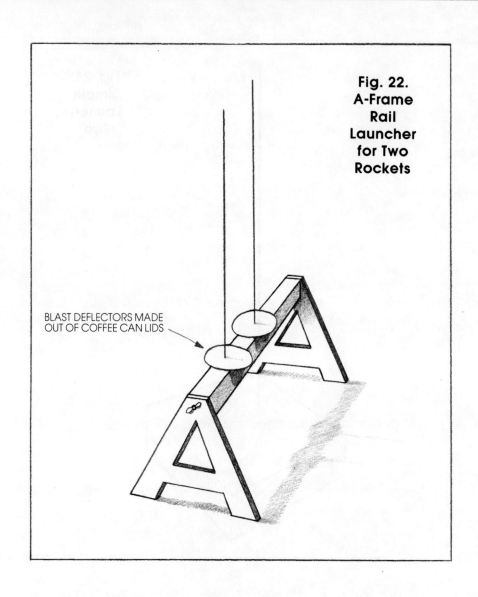

BLAST DEFLECTORS MADE OUT OF COFFEE CAN LIDS

Fig. 22.
A-Frame
Rail
Launcher
for Two
Rockets

a food can that has had its top and bottom removed and been cut with a metal snip along one side. The can is bent so that the engine exhaust is deflected to one side during a launch. This is basically what is done with large launch vehicles such as the Space Shuttle.

The principal advantage of this launch pad is simplicity, but its disadvantage is that it is difficult to use on windy days. Recovering a rocket on a windy day is a chancy business. It is best to tilt the launch rod so that the rocket is aimed into the wind. Thus, when the rocket returns, the wind should cause it to drift back to the launch pad. Pointing the pad into the wind is tricky because one side has to be elevated with pieces of wood or stones, and this makes it unstable for launch. The pad might tip over as the rocket is fired.

A second kind of launcher, an A-frame, can solve the pointing problem. (See Fig. 22.) This type of launcher looks like a sawhorse, but the crosspiece can be tilted at will. Machine bolts are imbedded into the ends of the crosspiece, and these pass through the A-frames. Wing nuts tighten the frames to the crosspiece. When the wind is blowing, the entire launcher is turned perpendicular to the wind, and the crosspiece is tilted and tightened.

A-frame launchers can be made with a long crosspiece that can accommodate several rods for multiple launchings. In this case, the pad is called a rail launcher.

One other launch pad design features three metal rods that are imbedded into some plaster of paris or cement that has been allowed to harden inside a coffee can. The rods are spaced just far enough from each other so that a rocket of a particular body diameter can fit neatly between them. (See Fig. 23.)

With this kind of launch pad, known as a tower launcher, rockets do not need a launch lug. Rocketeers have estimated that launch lugs cut down by about 15 percent the rocket's performance due to friction with the launch rod and the air. Tower launchers give higher altitude performance to

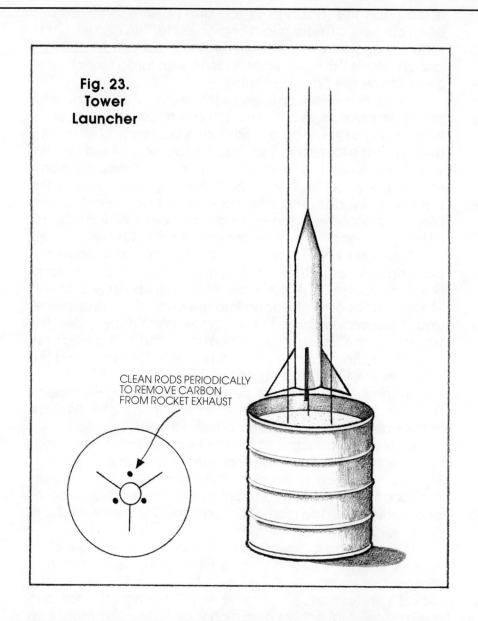

**Fig. 23.
Tower
Launcher**

CLEAN RODS PERIODICALLY
TO REMOVE CARBON
FROM ROCKET EXHAUST

rockets, but they can be used with only one size rocket or body tube. Additional tower launchers have to be built for rockets with different size body tubes. Also, the rods need to be cleaned of carbon buildup from the rocket exhaust. Spray lubricants are used to make the rods as slippery as possible. Another disadvantage with tower launchers is that they must be pointed the same way that the first pad is pointed. Tower launchers are best reserved for windless days when high-altitude flights are desired.

CONTROL PANEL

One of the important safety aspects of model rocketry is the launch control panel. Trying to fire a rocket with a match and fuse can lead to premature ignition and possible injury. Never do this. Proper launch ignition is done electrically. Before erecting the rocket on the pad, an igniter wire is inserted into the nozzle of the engine. The ends of the wire are then attached to wires from the control panel with small alligator clips. At the correct moment, electricity from a six-volt battery or a combination of batteries heats the igniter until it becomes red-hot. A chemical that coats the middle of the wire burns and this, in turn, ignites the engine. For fail-safe ignition, the igniter wire should be in direct contact with the engine propellant.

For safety, control panels have two switches that must be turned on in order to ignite the engine. The first switch is the safety switch. This switch is wired into a small light that turns on when the switch is "armed." The second switch is a push button of the type that is used for doorbells. This is the switch that actually fires the rocket. (See Fig. 24.)

RECOVERY

One of the advantages of model rockets over most full-scale rockets used by governments and private industry is that

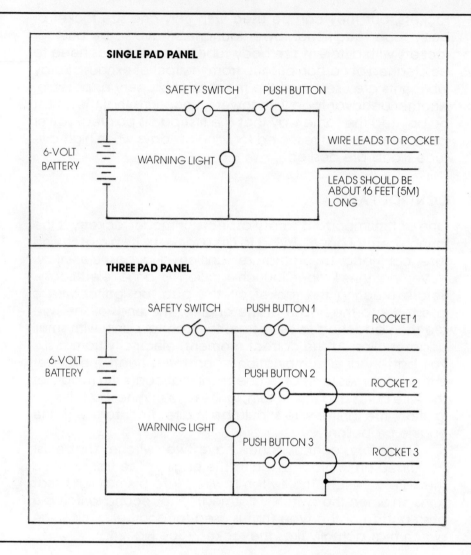

Fig. 24. Control Panel Wiring

they are reusable. After the rocket returns to the ground, the used engine can be replaced with a new engine for another flight. By using one of many recovery systems, the rocket can be returned to the ground far slower than when it left and used many times over.

Some of the earliest model rockets ever flown used a tumble recovery system. A small metal clip was mounted to the outside of the body tube that would catch the rocket engine after the ejection charge was fired. The engine would slide back a short distance, and this would upset the rocket's stability. The center of mass was moved to the center of pressure, and this caused the rocket to tumble as it fell. Tumbling made it return to the ground much slower than if it had fallen arrowlike. Careful aiming of the landing sight was necessary with this rocket because if it fell on hard ground, the fins would usually be broken by the force of impact.

Another early recovery system let the engine case be completely ejected from the rocket, and the rocket would then fall arrowlike to the ground. This system is used only with very lightweight rockets that have rounded nose cones. Heavier, pointed rockets become dangerous when they return, and often the tip of the nose cone is crushed on impact.

Other recovery systems rely on the engine ejection charge separating the nose from the body tube and, at the same time, pushing out a plastic streamer or parachute. With the nose cone separated from the body tube, although still held by an elastic shock cord, the rocket is unstable and begins to tumble back to the earth. A paper or plastic streamer attached to the shock cord increases the vehicle's drag. This has the effect of slowing its fall. Streamers are usually brightly colored. This helps the model rocketeer to follow the vehicle by eyesight on its way back down. Parachutes provide the slowest and safest recovery for the vehicle, but there is one big disadvantage to their use. On windy days, the returning rocket may be blown quite some distance before it touches down, and many rockets have been lost when they drifted into distant trees. One way of solving this problem is to cut a hole in the top of the parachute canopy. This will speed up the rocket's return to the ground.

Advanced rocket modelers experiment with glider recovery by adding wings to their rocket. This kind of rocket is called a booster glider, and it takes much skill and experience to design one that is successful both during launch and during recovery. (See Fig. 25.) Another advanced recovery system has small blades that resemble the rotors of a helicopter as they rotate toward the ground.

Fig. 25. Boost Glide Recovery

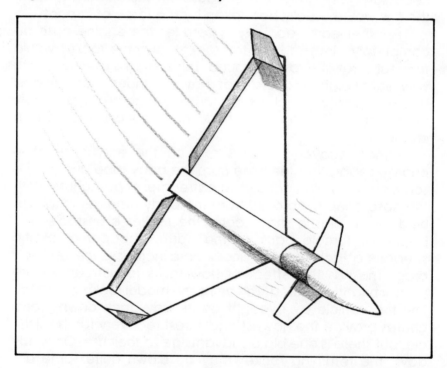

ADVANCED ROCKETRY

Rocket kits are a good way to get started on model rocketry. After a while, however, many rocketeers start to create their own designs. Supply companies provide parts such as body tubes and nose cones in a wide variety of sizes to suit almost any experiment. Also, rockets that have been wrecked in flight can be saved for spare parts.

Advanced rocket projects include multiple-stage vehicles, payloads such as cameras that photograph the ground from high altitudes, cluster-engine vehicles, boost gliders, and scale models. The last category, scale models, require a high degree of model-making skill. Kits that replicate actual launch vehicles, such as the Saturn V, are very expensive and difficult to build. However, if finished properly, they make beautiful display models and produce spectacular flights. It is best to save these kits for building after you have become an experienced modeler. Start with simpler, less expensive kits.

MODEL ROCKET CLUBS

In many parts of the United States and the rest of the world, model rocketry has been organized into clubs. Clubs promote rocket safety and join together people who have a similar interest. In model rocket clubs, members have the advantage of working with experienced modelers and quickly learn a great deal about the hobby of building and flying rockets. Clubs also sponsor flying events where members can show off their skills. Competitions for high-altitude flights, new designs, and scale-model building add great interest and excitement to model rocketry.

Check with your library or teachers at school to find out if there are any local rocketry clubs. If no clubs exist in your area, consider forming one. Model rocketry manufacturers are anxious to promote their products and will gladly provide information to people who want to start clubs. Invite a teacher from your school or another interested adult to become a club sponsor and write these companies for an information package.

Also, you might consider becoming a member of the National Association of Rocketry (NAR), a nonprofit group of hobbyists that provides information on contests and records and publishes the only monthly magazine on model rocketry in existence. NAR also insures its members and has worked to remove restrictive laws that classify model rockets as fireworks and thus forbid their use.

SAFETY

Since commercially built engines appeared for model rockets, there have been millions of rocket launches without a mishap. Part of the credit for this safety record lies with the instrinsic safeness of the engine design. The rest of the credit goes to following a carefully devised set of safety procedures. A model rocketry code has been developed that is so safe that, when followed exactly, accidents are extremely unlikely. That code—approved by model manufacturers, hobby industries, and rocketry clubs—is reproduced here for you to use. Study it carefully and follow it. Then model rocketry will become an exciting but safe hobby and sport for you, too.

Model Rocketry Safety Code

1.Construction—My model rockets will be made of lightweight materials such as paper, wood, plastic, and rubber, without any metal as structural parts.

2.Engines—I will use only preloaded factory-made model rocket engines in the manner recommended by the manufacturer. I will not change in any way nor attempt to reload these engines.

3. Recovery—I will always use a recovery system in my model rockets that will return them safely to the ground so that they may be flown again.

4. Weight Limits—My model rocket will weigh no more than 453 grams (16 ounces) at lift off, and the engines will contain no more than 113 grams (4 ounces) of propellant.

5. Stability—I will check the stability of my model rockets before their first flight, except when launching models of already proven stability.

6. Launching System—The system I use to launch my model rockets must be remotely controlled and electrically operated, and will contain a switch that will return to "off" when released. I will remain at least 15 feet (4.5 m) away from any rocket that is being launched.

7. Launch Safety—I will not let anyone approach a model rocket on a launcher until I have made sure that either the safety interlock key has been removed or the battery has been disconnected from my launcher.

8. Flying Conditions—I will not launch my model rockets in high winds, near buildings, power lines, tall trees, low-flying aircraft, or under any conditions that might be dangerous to people or property.

9. Launch Area—My model rockets will always be launched from a cleared area, free of any easy to burn materials, and I will only use nonflammable recovery wadding in my rockets.

10. Jet Deflector—My launcher will have a jet deflector device to prevent the engine exhaust from hitting the ground directly.

11. Launch Rod—To prevent accidental eye injury, I will always place the launcher so the end of the rod is above eye level, or cap the end of the rod with my hand when approaching it. I will never place my head or body over the launching rod. When my launcher is not in use, I will always store it so that the launch rod is *not* in an upright position.

12. Power Lines—I will never attempt to recover my model rocket from a power line or other dangerous place.

13. Launch Targets and Angle—I will not launch rockets so their flight path will carry them against targets on the ground, and will never use an explosive warhead nor a payload that is intended to be flammable. My launching device will always be pointed within 30 degrees of vertical.

14. Prelaunch Test—When conducting research activities with unproven designs or methods, I will, when possible, determine their reliability through prelaunch tests. I will conduct launchings of unproven designs in complete isolation from persons not participating in the actual launching.

FOR SUPPLIES OR
MORE INFORMATION

FOR SUPPLIES

Celestial Enterprises
4412 Crabapple
Ft. Worth, TX 76137

Celestial is a small company that carries several unique products, including some unusual kits and several sizes of strong
cloth parachutes.

Centuri Engineering
Box 1988
Phoenix, AZ 85001

Centuri is noted for the innovative designs and quality of their
kits, especially scale-model rockets.

CNA Systems
37 High Street
Lewiston, ME 04248

CNA specializes in the application of electronics to rocketry. Science projects and technical experiments can be based on their products.

Competition Model Rockets
7206 Beechwood Road
Alexandria, VA 22307

CMR specializes in materials and kits to win NAR-sanctioned contests. They are well known for their imaginative products.

Estes Industries
Penrose, CO 81240

Estes is the largest of the major model-rocket manufacturers and has the largest selection of kits and materials.

Flight Systems, Inc.
9300 E. 68th Street
Raytown, MO 64133

Flight Systems manufacture a complete line of kits and the largest selection of rocket engines of different thrusts available.

FOR INFORMATION

National Association of Rocketry
182 Madison Drive
Elizabeth, PA 15037

This national, nonprofit organization sanctions meets, insures its members, works with public services, and publishes the monthly *Model Rocketeer* magazine.

INDEX